MODERN MILITARY AIRCRAFT

MODERN
MILITARY
AIRCRAFT

MARTIN BOWMAN

CHARTWELL BOOKS INC.

A BISON BOOK

First published in the United States by
Chartwell Books Inc.
A Division of Book Sales Inc.
110 Enterprise Avenue
Secaucus, New Jersey 07094

Copyright © 1980
Bison Books Limited

Produced by Bison Books Limited
4 Cromwell Place
London SW7

ISBN 0 89009 312 1
Library of Congress Catalog Card
Number 79 91471
Printed in Singapore

CONTENTS

INTRODUCTION

Many of the aircraft featured in *Modern Military Aircraft* are not modern at all. However, their avionics and weaponry are. Aircraft such as the B-52, Vulcan, Shackleton, Delta Dart and the F-4 Phantom, to name but a few, have had their operational lives extended with the introduction of advanced navigational, radar and Electrical Counter Measures (ECM) systems, stand-off bombs and sophisticated Short-Range Attack and Air Launch Cruise missiles. It is hard to believe that aircraft such as the F-4 Phantom and the redoubtable Lockheed Hercules have been around since the late 1950s. Ever increasing defense costs have prolonged the life of other aircraft like the

BAC Canberra bomber, which first flew in 1949, and the F-106 Delta Dart which first flew in 1956 will remain in service with the RAF and USAF until the 1980s. The Dassault Mirage IV, shown on this page, is a limited range strategic bomber, which first flew in 1959. It is typical of the material contained throughout this all-color book. Although at first glance some aircraft appear outside the scope of this book, they are in fact worthy of inclusion.

In all about 160 aircraft are featured, although for the most part Russian military aircraft have been excluded because of the lack of suitable color material. Many of the specially selected pictures are masterpieces

of photography and the text is but a frame in which to display them.

Among the aircraft featured are the most advanced in the world. The F-14 and F-15 fighters are illustrated as well as the proto-type B-1 bomber.

Assembling the photographs proved difficult and I am most grateful to all the aircraft companies who very kindly contributed material. I would also like to thank Erol A Araf, Harry Gann, Harry Holmes, Anthony Lewis, Rob Mack, Paul R Maurice, Geoffrey Norris, James Ragsdale, William H Schmidt, Don White, Gordon S Williams and Wofram Wolff for all the considerable work they have put in on my behalf. Without all of them this book would not have been possible.

Martin W Bowman.

FIGHTERS,GROUND ATTACK AIRCRAFT

Toward the end of World War II German jet fighters such as the Me 262 and rocket fighters like the Komet were regularly seen by Allied bomber crews. Britain was not far behind in jet-fighter design and had gained a world lead by 1945 with the Gloster Meteor. Within six months of the end of the war the Meteor had raised the World Absolute Speed Record to the incredible figure of 606 mph. Britain's lead in fighter design was not seriously challenged by America until 1947. On 1 October that year the North American XP-86, which had benefited from German research into swept-wings, flew for

the first time. In the spring of 1948 during a shallow dive, it became the first aircraft to exceed the speed of sound. A year later the F-86 Sabre (1), as it became known, established a new World Air Speed Record of 671 mph.

During the Korean War F-86Es and F-86Fs proved highly successful in combats with MiG-15s despite the American fighter's inferior climbing and altitude performance. On 17 December 1950 four MiG-15s were reported destroyed in the first recorded dog-fight between F-86 Sabres and MiG jet fighters.

In August 1975 almost all 31 Hawker Siddeley Andover C Mk 1 tactical transports (*49*), acquired in 1966, were withdrawn from RAF Air Support Command. Six have been converted for radio and radar calibration duties and one serves with No 32 Squadron together with this unit's CC Mk 2s and the Queen's Flight (*49A*). The Andover C Mk 1 was slightly larger and much heavier than the HS 748 civil version but it could operate from 300-yard airstrips and could carry up to 58 troops or 14,000 lbs of cargo.

The Italian Air Force's most important tactical transport is the Aeritalia G.222 which first flew on 18 July 1970. This V/STOL transport originated from a NATO specification in the early 1960s. In December 1975 the Italian Air Force began receiving the first of 44 G.222s but the only other orders have come from the United Arab Emirates (Dubai) and the Argentine Navy (*50*).

Similar in design is the AG Transall C-160 tactical transport (*51, 51A*) designed by Transporter Allianz as a replacement for the veteran Nord Noratlas. The Allianz was formed in 1959 by what are known today as Aerospatiale of France, MBB of West Germany and VFW-Fokker (West Germany/Netherlands). On 25 February 1963 the C-160 flew for the first time. Although it has proved more successful than the G.222, with exports to South Africa and Turkey, it still remains, as does the G.222, in the shadow of the more famous and yet more illustrious C-130 Hercules airplane.

50

51

51A

The McDonnell Douglas C-9 Nightingale (*52, 52A*) is another military transport developed from a civil airliner, in this case, the DC-9. The Nightingale serves in three main roles: aeromedical airlift, special executive transport (VC-9C) and passenger-cargo transport (C-9B). The flying hospital can carry 30 litter patients or 40 ambulatory patients in addition to attendants.

Israel Aircraft Industries' 201 Arava light STOL transport and utility aircraft is also a military version of a civil aircraft. It has a flight crew of one or two and can carry up to 24 fully equipped troops or 16 paratroops and two despatchers or 12 litter patients and two attendants. The Arava 202 (*53*) has uprated turboprop engines and incorporates Whitcomb winglets and a wet wing. Search and rescue, maritime patrol and surveillance versions of this airplane are being proposed for the future.

52

52A

Japan's contribution in the transport stakes is the turbofan-powered Kawasaki C-1A medium-range transport (54) which equips the Japanese Self-Defense Force. Designed in 1946 as a replacement for the C-46 Curtiss Commando, the C-1 first flew on 12 November 1970 and entered service in December 1974. The Japanese have taken a leaf out of the European's book and formed a consortium of Japanese companies to produce the C-1A with Kawasaki as main contractor.

De Havilland (Canada) has developed two excellent STOL tactical transports in the DHC-4 Caribou (55) and the DHC-5 Buffalo (56). The Caribou first flew on 30 July 1958 and five were delivered for evaluation by the US Army in August 1959. Subsequently, 159 heavier versions were delivered and the type saw widespread service during the Vietnam War. By 1975 more than 330 had been built and now serve with 14 different nations although Canada is not one of them. Its success led to the develop-

ment of the Buffalo which was accepted by the US Army after competing against 24 other contenders for a STOL tactical transport. The Buffalo first flew on 9 April 1964 and when production temporarily ceased in 1972, 59 had been built. Two years later production was restarted and total production will exceed 100.

The Short Skyvan 3M (57) is another transport with excellent STOL performance. A derivative of the civil aircraft, it first flew in early 1970 and operates in 12 different nations. Its biggest customer is the Sultan of Oman's Air Force which has 16 aircraft. The Skyvan is capable of carrying 22 troops or 12 stretcher cases and two medical attendants and has a full-section rear door for parachutists and dropping loads in flight. It can also fulfill a multitude of roles including multi-sensor reconnaissance and search and rescue. However this type is so far not being considered for operations with the RAF.

54

119

120

Italy's aerobatic display team, the Frecce Tricolori, uses the Fiat G.91 PAN, seen here overflying a USAF SR-71 Blackbird (*118*). The Italian display team has given many colorful displays in Europe and has been a regular visitor to England in recent years. The two photographs show (*119*) a line-up of Fiat G.91s at a display at RAF Mildenhall and another being refuelled (*120*) with a Vulcan from No 617, "The Dambusters," Squadron, in the background. It was during this display, in June 1979, that one of these machines touched a tree and crashed, killing the pilot. The Red Arrows have had their fatal accidents too but let us hope that all these magnificent display teams continue to entertain the public, safely and spectacularly, for many more years to come.

118

TRAINERS AND UTILITY AIRCRAFT

Although most of the world's air forces have completed the transition from propeller to jet combat-aircraft, basic flying training is still taught on propeller-driven aircraft for economy and safety reasons. The first 100 hours of military flying training, especially if they include time on jet aircraft, are among the most expensive. The failure rate can be as high as 50 percent of the intake.

Thus, air staffs look to low-cost trainers with jet aircraft performance like the Rhein-Flugzeugbau (VFW-Fokker) Fantrainer (*121*) whose concept is based on the integrated ducted-fan propulsion system. The first prototype was powered by two coupled Wankel rotary engines of 150 hp each. The series version undergoing flight testing is powered by a turboshaft engine of 400 hp.

Ab initio advanced flying training is the all-important first step for any aspiring pilot and the RAF has always been well supplied with a number of successful designs starting with the Avro 504K in the 1930s. The last piston-engined basic trainer to enter RAF service was the Percival Provost in 1953. Two years later it was replaced by the RAF's first-ever jet trainer, the BAC (originally Hunting) Jet Provost derivative (*122*). It still plays an important role in training programs. The unpressurized T Mk 3A and the pressurized T Mk 5A serve at the RAF College, Cranwell and others of varying marks serve at RAF flying schools throughout the UK (*123*).

122

123

121

From this BAC developed the 145 multi-role trainer-attack aircraft which was later developed into the Strikemaster light tactical/trainer. It has set a world record for the number of repeat orders placed and among its customers are the Royal Saudi Air Force, which flies the Mk 80 (*124*), the Royal New Zealand Air Force (Mk 88) (*125*) and the Royal Malaysian Air Force (*126*). The latter is one of seven Air Forces outside the United Kingdom which uses the Scottish Aviation SA-3 Bulldog (*127*) primary trainer. The Beagle-designed Bulldog entered service in 1973 and is used in Britain chiefly by 16 University Air Squadrons across the country.

125

124

127

From 1962 until 1977 the RAF's standard advanced trainer was the Folland-designed Hawker Siddeley Gnat. It has been replaced by the Hawker Siddeley Hawk T Mk 1 two-seat multi-purpose trainer (*128*) which was first introduced at the end of 1976. By 1978 it had totally replaced the Gnat in the advanced training role and in 1980, replaced the Gnat as the Red Arrows' aircraft. The Hawk, pictured here displaying its 30 mm Aden gun pack and two Sidewinder AAMs (*129*), has also begun replacing the Hunter T7 (*130*) in the weapons' training role. Single-seat and two-seat ground attack versions are being offered for export (*131*).

131

The Hawk faces tough competition from the Dassault-Breguet-Dornier Alpha Jet (*132*) trainer/light strike-reconnaissance aircraft which is among competitors for the US Navy's VT-X program for 350 trainer aircraft to replace the TA-4J Skyhawk.

The original Cessna T-37A was the first USAF jet trainer designed as such from the start. From November 1959 deliveries switched to the T-37B and all T-37A models were modified to B standard. When production ceased in 1975 more than 1300 had been delivered to the USAF and 14 other countries. Some 680 are still in service with the US Air Training Command. Cessna restressed the airframe and supplanted uprated J85 turbojets to create the A-37 Dragonfly (*133*) two-seat strike aircraft. About 511 were built and many were used in Southeast Asia. Others have been delivered to foreign Air Forces, mainly in Latin America.

The transformation work had begun during the 1960s at a time when there was a rekindling of interest in Co-in (counterinsurgency) aircraft needed to dampen down "brushfire wars." As a result, the North American (Rockwell) OV-10 Bronco

14807

was ordered into production for the USMC and USAF in 1966 for counter-insurgency operations. Service deliveries began in February 1968 and the Bronco made its operational debut with the USMC in Vietnam in July 1968.

Among the oldest trainers in service is the Lockheed T-33 which first flew in 1948. About 800 still serve with over 30 countries in the AT-33 and RT-33 configuration. In all 6557 were built.

In 1960 Canadair produced and flew the CL-41 Tutor basic trainer. The RCAF (later called Canadian Armed Forces) took delivery of the first of 190 models in 1963 for pilot training. The model pictured (*134*) is a CL 41G which also equips two Royal Malaysian Air Force units.

Another basic trainer which has been around for a long time is the Potez-Air Fouga (Aerospatiale) Magister. It flew for the first time on 23 July 1952 and after prolonged development was put into production for the French Air Force and the French Navy, beginning in February 1956. Other versions have been built abroad and just over 50 were ordered by Israel. The Heyl Ha'Avir used the Magister during the Six-Day War of June 1967 and this has led to limited use in COIN operations, especially in Africa where it serves with five Air Forces in the armed trainer role.

140

The Fouga 90 (*135*) is an Aerospatiale pri-
vate venture project based on the successful
Magister design. It has a more spacious
cockpit, turbofan engines which are claimed
to offer a 50 percent improvement in fuel
consumption over the Magister and is designed to meet the needs of Air Forces with
limited budgets.

135

Another cost-effective trainer is the Aermacchi M.B. 339 development of the 326 basic trainer, light attack aircraft. The M.B. 339 has modern stepped cockpits like the HSA Hawk and is powered by a Rolls-Royce Viper single-shaft turbojet. Variants of the M.B. 326 (*136*) are in service with a dozen different countries and the M.B. 339 is already under production for the Italian Air Force.